STUDY GUIDE

Holes

Louis Sachar

WITH CONNECTIONS

HOLT, RINEHART AND WINSTON

A Harcourt Classroom Education Company

Austin · New York · Orlando · Atlanta · San Francisco · Boston · Dallas · Toronto · London

Staff Credits

Vice-President: Mescal Evler

Manager of Editorial Operations: Bill Wahlgren

Executive Editor: Katie Vignery

Book Editor: Carolyn Logan

Editorial Staff: *Assistant Managing Editor,* Marie Price; *Editorial Operations Coordinator,* Lori De La Garza; *Copyediting Manager,* Michael Neibergall; *Copyediting Supervisor,* Mary Malone; *Copyeditors,* Joel Bourgeois, Liz Dickson, Emily Force, Julie Hill, Julia Hu, Jennifer Kirkland, Millicent Ondras, Dennis Scharnberg; *Editorial Coordinator,* Mark Holland; *Assistant Editorial Coordinator,* Heather Cheyne; *Editorial Coordinators,* Diane Hardin, Marcus Johnson, Janet Riley, Kelly Tankersley; *Word Processors,* Ruth Hooker, Joie Pickett, Margaret Sanchez

Permissions: Carrie Jones

Design: *Design Director,* Curtis Riker; *Art Buyer Supervisor,* Elaine Tate

Prepress Production: Beth Prevelige, Gene Rumann, Carol Trammel

Manufacturing Coordinator: Shirley Cantrell

Electronic Publishing: *Operators,* JoAnn Brown, Lana Knapp, Indira Konanur, Christopher Lucas, Nanda Patel; *Administrative Coordinator,* Sally Williams

For permission to reprint copyrighted material, grateful acknowledgment is made to the following source:

Farrar, Straus and Giroux, LLC: From *Holes* by Louis Sachar. Copyright © 1998 by Louis Sachar.

Cover: Sally Vitsky/Artco LLC

HRW is a trademark licensed to Holt, Rinehart and Winston registered in the United States of America and/or other jurisdictions.

Printed in the United States of America

ISBN 0-03-066413-6

3456 085 05 04 03 02

TABLE *of* CONTENTS

Using This Study Guide

This Study Guide is intended to

- *provide maximum versatility and flexibility*
- *serve as a ready resource for background information on both the author and the book*
- *act as a catalyst for discussion, analysis, interpretation, activities, and further research*
- *provide reproducible masters that can be used for either individual or collaborative work, including discussions and projects*
- *provide multiple options for evaluating students' progress through the novel and the Connections*

Literary Elements

- plot structure
- major themes
- characterization
- setting
- point of view
- symbolism, irony, and other elements appropriate to the title

Making Meanings Reproducible Masters

- First Thoughts
- Shaping Interpretations
- Connecting with the Text
- Extending the Text
- Challenging the Text

A **Reading Check** focuses on review and comprehension.

The Worksheets Reproducible Masters

- Reading Strategies Worksheets
- Literary Elements Worksheets
- Vocabulary Worksheets

Approaching the Novel

The successful study of a novel often depends on students' enthusiasm, curiosity, and openness. The ideas in **Introducing the Novel** will help you create such a climate for your class. Background information in **About the Writer** and **About the Novel** can also be used to pique students' interest.

Reading and Responding to the Novel

Making Meanings questions are designed for both individual response and group or class discussion. They range from personal response to high-level critical thinking.

Reading Strategies worksheets contain graphic organizers. They help students explore techniques that enhance both comprehension and literary analysis. Many worksheets are appropriate for more than one set of chapters.

Novel Notes provide high-interest information relating to historical, cultural, literary, and other elements of the novel. The **Investigate** questions and **Reader's Log** ideas guide students to further research and consideration.

Choices suggest a wide variety of activities for exploring different aspects of the novel, either individually or collaboratively. The results may be included in a portfolio or used as springboards for larger projects.

The **Glossary and Vocabulary** list (1) clarifies allusions and other references and (2) provides definitions students may refer to as they read. The **Vocabulary Worksheets** activities are based on the Vocabulary Words.

Reader's Log, Double-Entry Journal, and **Group Discussion Log** model formats and spark ideas for responding to the novel. These pages are designed to be a resource for independent reading as well.

Responding to the Novel as a Whole

The following features provide options for culminating activities that can be used in whole-class, small-group, or independent-study situations.

Novel Review provides a format for summarizing and integrating the major literary elements.

Novel Projects suggest multiple options for culminating activities. **Writing About the Novel, Cross-Curricular Connections,** and **Multimedia and Internet Connections** propose project options that extend the text into other genres, content areas, and environments.

Responding to the Connections

Making Meanings questions in **Exploring the Connections** facilitate discussion of the additional readings in the HRW LIBRARY edition of this novel.

Tips for Classroom Management

Preparing Students for Reading

Set aside a time each week for talking about books. On the right are some ideas for introducing a novel and motivating students to pick it up and begin reading.

Reading and Responding

Book groups Although most students will read independently, discussions with classmates can enrich their reading enormously. This Study Guide suggests appropriate points to stop and talk about the story so far. At these stopping points, the **Making Meanings** questions can be used as discussion starters. Ask groups to keep a simple log of their discussions.

Full-class discussions Engage students by beginning the discussion with a question that encourages a personal response (see **First Thoughts** in **Making Meanings**). As students respond to the questions involving interpretation, invite them to support their inferences and conclusions with evidence from the text. Encourage a noncritical environment. Show your own enthusiasm for the novel—it's infectious!

Reader's logs Logs, journals, and notebooks offer an open and nonthreatening yet systematic mode for students to respond in writing to the novel. Making entries as they read can help students learn more about themselves as readers, monitor their own progress, and write more easily and fluently. Keeping logs can also enhance participation in small-group and class discussions of the novel. Consider dialogue journals in which two readers—a student and you, a classmate, or a family member—exchange thoughts about their reading. **Reader's Log** suggestions appear in each issue of **Novel Notes.**

Cooperative learning Small groups may meet both to discuss the novel and to plan and work on projects related to the novel (see ideas in **Choices** and in **Novel Projects**). Encourage full participation by making sure that each group member has a defined role and that the roles rotate so that the same student is not always the leader or the recorder, for example.

Projects While students' projects can extend into other content areas, they should always contribute to enriching and extending students' understanding of the novel itself. If students know when they begin the novel that presenting a project will be a part of their evaluation, they can begin early to brainstorm, discuss, and try out ideas. Project ideas can come from **Novel Notes,** from the **Choices** activities, from the **Novel Projects** ideas, and, of course, from the students themselves. Projects can be developed and presented by individuals, pairs, or groups.

Reflecting

When students finish the novel, they should not be left with a test as the culminating experience. Project presentations can be a kind of celebration, as can a concluding discussion. On the right are some ideas for a reflective discussion. They can be used in a whole-class environment, or small groups can choose certain questions to answer and share their conclusions (or their disagreements) with the class.

Ideas for Introducing the Novel

- Give a brief book talk to arouse students' curiosity and interest (see **About the Novel** for ideas).

- Play or show a segment of an audio, film, or video version of the book or an interview with the writer.

- Present high-interest biographical information about the writer (see **About the Writer** in this Study Guide and the biographical sketch at the end of the HRW Library edition of this novel).

- Read aloud a passage from the novel that arouses your own interest, and elicit predictions, inferences, and speculations from students.

- Lead a focused class discussion or suggest activities that (1) draw on students' prior knowledge or (2) lead them to generate their own ideas about a significant topic or theme they will encounter in the novel (see **Before You Read).**

Reader's Log Starters

- When I began reading this book, I thought…
- My favorite part, so far, is…
- I predict that…
- I like the way the writer…
- I'd like to ask the writer…
- If I had written this book, I would have…
- This [character, incident, idea] reminds me of …
- This book made me think about…
- This book made me realize…

Questions for Reflection

- What was your favorite part of the book (and why)?

- If you could be one of the characters, who would it be (and why)?

- Would you or wouldn't you recommend this book to a friend (and why)?

- What is the most important thing about this book?

- Would you change the ending? If not, what makes it work? If yes, what changes would you make?

- If you could have a conversation with the writer, what would you say or ask?

Strategies for Inclusion

Each set of activities has been developed to meet special student interests, abilities, and learning styles. Because the questions and activities in this Study Guide are directed to the students, there are no labels to indicate the types of learners they target. However, in each Before You Read, Choices, *and* Novel Projects *page, you will find activities to meet the needs of*

- *less proficient readers*
- *students acquiring English*
- *advanced students*

The activities and projects have been prepared to accommodate these different learning styles:

- *auditory/musical*
- *interpersonal*
- *intrapersonal*
- *kinesthetic*
- *logical/mathematical*
- *verbal/linguistic*
- *visual/spatial*

Using the Study Guide Questions and Activities

Encourage students to adapt the suggestions given in the Study Guide to fit their own learning styles and interests. It is important to remember that students are full of surprises, and a question or activity that is challenging to an advanced student can also be handled successfully by students who are less proficient readers. The high interest level, flexibility, and variety of these questions and activities make them appropriate for a range of students.

Students should be encouraged to vary the types of activities they choose so that the same student is not regularly selecting writing or researching activities over those involving speaking, art, and performing, and vice versa. Individual and group work should also alternate so that students have the opportunity to work on their own and as part of collaborative learning groups.

Working in Pairs and Groups

When students with varying abilities, cultural backgrounds, and learning styles work together, they can arrive at a deeper understanding of both the novel and one another.

Reading pairs can stop and check each other's responses to the novel at frequent intervals.

Students from different cultural groups can interview one another about how certain situations, character interactions, character motivations, and so on would be viewed in their home cultures.

Visualizing and Performing

Students who have difficulty with writing or with presenting their ideas orally can demonstrate their understanding of the novel in a variety of ways:

- making cluster diagrams or sketching their ideas

- creating tableaux showing where characters are in relation to one another during a scene, their poses or stances, and their facial expressions

- creating thought balloons with drawings or phrases that show what a character is thinking at a given moment

- drawing their own thoughts in thought balloons above a sketched self-portrait

- listing or drawing images that come to mind as they read or hear a certain section or passage of the novel

- making a comic-book version of the novel (with or without words)

- coming to class as a character in the novel

Assessment Options

Perhaps the most important goal of assessment is to inform instruction. As you monitor the degree to which your students understand and engage with the book, you will naturally modify your instructional plan. The frequency and balance of class and small-group discussion, the time allowed for activities, and the extent to which direct teaching of reading skills and strategies, literary elements, or vocabulary is appropriate can all be planned on the basis of your ongoing assessment of your students' needs.

Several forms of assessment are particularly appropriate for work with the book:

Observing and note taking Anecdotal records that reflect both the degree and the quality of students' participation in class and small-group discussions and activities will help you target areas in which coaching or intervention is appropriate. Because communication skills are such an integral part of working with the book in a classroom setting, it is appropriate to evaluate the process of making meaning in this social context.

Involving yourself with dialogue journals and letters You may want to exchange notes with students instead of, or in addition to, encouraging them to keep reader's logs. A powerful advantage of this strategy is that at the same time you have the opportunity to evaluate students' responses, you can make a significant difference in the quality of the response. When students are aware that their comments are valued (and addressed to a real audience, an audience that writes back), they often wake up to the significance of what they are reading and begin to make stronger connections between the text and their own lives.

Agreeing on criteria for evaluation If evaluation is to be fair, it must be predictable. As students propose and plan an activity or project, collaborate with them to set up the criteria by which their work will be evaluated, and be consistent in applying only those criteria.

Encouraging self-evaluation and goal setting When students are partners with you in creating criteria for evaluation, they can apply those criteria to their own work. You might ask them to rate themselves on a simple scale of 1, 2, or 3 for each of the criteria and to arrive at an overall score. Students can then set goals based on self-evaluation.

Peer evaluation Students can participate in evaluating one another's demonstrations and presentations, basing their evaluations upon a previously established set of standards. Modeling a peer-evaluation session will help students learn this method, and a chart or checklist can guide peer discussion. Encourage students to be objective, sensitive, courteous, and constructive in their comments.

Keeping portfolios If you are in an environment where portfolios contain only carefully chosen samples of students' writing, you may want to introduce a second "working" portfolio and negotiate grades with students after examining all or selected items from these portfolios.

Opportunities for Assessment

The suggestions in this Study Guide provide multiple opportunities for assessment across a range of skills:

- demonstrating reading comprehension
- keeping reader's logs
- listening and speaking
- working in groups—both discussion and activity oriented
- planning, developing, and presenting a final project
- acquiring vocabulary
- taking tests

Questions for Self-evaluation and Goal Setting

- What are the three most important things I learned in my work with this book?
- How will I follow up with these so that I remember them?
- What was the most difficult part of working with this book?
- How did I deal with the difficulty, and what would I do differently?
- What two goals will I work toward in my reading/writing/group work?
- What steps will I take to achieve those goals?

Items for a "Working" Portfolio

- reading records
- drafts of written work and project plans
- audio- and videotapes of presentations
- notes on discussions
- reminders of cooperative projects, such as planning and discussion notes
- artwork
- objects and mementos connected with themes and topics in the book
- other evidence of engagement with the book

For help with establishing and maintaining portfolio assessment, examine the **Portfolio Management System** in **Elements of Literature.**

About the Writer

Louis Sachar

More on Sachar

Hearne, Betsy. "He Didn't Do It." *The New York Times Review of Books,* November 15, 1998, p. 52.

Strickland, Barbara. "An Austin Author's Sensible Success Story. Louis Sachar: Top of His Class." *The Austin Chronicle,* February 26–March 4, 1999.

Hedblad, Alan, editor. "Sachar, Louis." *Something About the Author.* Detroit: The Gale Group, 1999, volume 104, pp. 157–61.

Also by Sachar

Sideways Stories from Wayside School. New York: Knopf, 1978. These humorous short stories introduce the reader to the bizarre happenings, strange teachers, and fascinating students in the Wayside School series.

There's a Boy in the Girls' Bathroom. New York: Knopf, 1987. The tale of the transformation of a misfit into a fifth-grade success story through the efforts of a new school counselor.

The Boy Who Lost His Face. New York: Random House Sprinters, 1989. David believes that a curse has been laid on him. Whatever the cause, David has to work his way through some humiliating experiences before he gets his "face" back.

Dogs Don't Tell Jokes. New York: Knopf, 1991. Gary enters the talent show as a stand-up comedian, even though no-one laughs at his jokes.

A biography of Louis Sachar appears in Holes, *HRW LIBRARY Edition. You may wish to share this additional biographical information with your students.*

Although writing was always Louis Sachar's first love, it took a number of years and several changes of career before he could devote himself to it full time.

Sachar was born in East Meadow, New York, in 1954. When he was nine, he and his family moved to Tustin, California, just south of Los Angeles. At the time, Orange County was still full of orange groves, and Sachar remembers threading his way through the trees to get to school. In grade school Sachar was a good student and he excelled in math. He developed a love for reading in high school, and by college he had become so fond of Russian literature that he tried to learn the language so he could read his favorite authors in their native tongue. Sachar first attended college at Antioch in Ohio, but his father's death prompted him to move back to California so he could be closer to his mother. He stayed out of school for a semester, earning money selling Fuller Brushes door-to-door, a brief career he has described as a surprising success. Soon Sachar was back in school, enrolled at the University of California at Berkeley, and studying economics. It wasn't until his final year as an undergraduate, in 1976, that he began to write for children.

After college, he wrote at night and worked during the day as a shipping manager at a sweater factory. Although he quickly found a publisher for his first book, *Sideways Stories from Wayside School,* the money he earned wasn't enough to support him. He went back to school and continued to write while he worked on his law degree. His work as a lawyer paid the bills until 1989, when he gave it up to write full time.

Sachar sometimes draws his ideas for his fiction from personal experiences and from the people around him. The children in *Sideways Stories,* for example, are named after the students at Hillside Elementary School, where Sachar worked as a teacher's aide. He used his own nickname at the school, Louis the Yard Teacher, for another character in that book. His wife, Carla, who was an elementary school counselor when he met her, inspired the character of the counselor in his book *There's a Boy in the Girls' Bathroom.* And their daughter Sherre, who was four years old when Sachar began his Marvin Redpost series, was the inspiration for Marvin's four-year-old sister. Not all of his characters are based on people he knows. Many come wholly out of his imagination. The more bizarre and surprising he can make a story, the more interested he stays while writing. "I just try to write books that are fun to read," says Sachar. "I figure if I like them, (readers) will too."[1]

Sachar says he learned to write for children by reading books for adults. Among his favorite authors are Kurt Vonnegut, E. L. Doctorow, J. D. Salinger, Flannery O'Connor, Rex Stout, Katherine Paterson, E. B. White, Kazuo Ishiguro, Leo Tolstoy, and Feodor Dostoevski.

Even after more than twenty years of writing and almost two dozen books, Sachar is still awed by the process of creating a work of fiction. "I'm always amazed when I finish a book and realize, 'Hey, this actually is what I set out to do.'"[1]

[1]From "Louis Sachar: Top of His Class" by Barbara Strickland from *The Austin Chronicle Online,* accessed June 4, 2001, at http://www.auschron.com/issues/vol18/issue26/books.sachar.html.

About the Novel

Awards and Honors (A)

Holes has won both the 1999 Newbery Medal and the National Book Award. It has also received *The Boston Globe-Horn Book* Award.

Holes as been honored by the ALA as Best Book for Young Adults, Notable Children's Book, and Quick Pick for Young Adults. The *New York Times Book Review* has named *Holes* Notable Children's Book of the Year, and *Publishers Weekly* named it Best Book of the Year.

For Listening

Holes. Old Greenwich, CT: Listening Library, 1999. Three sound cassettes; complete and unabridged. Read by Kerry Beyer.

Louis Sachar had a definite inspiration for his complex and clever novel, *Holes*. Sachar had recently moved to Texas and was struck by the state's searing summers. He wanted to craft a character who would be forced to struggle under that same Texas sun, so he came up with Stanley Yelnats.

Sachar identified with his main character's plight, having to dig a futile, five-foot hole every day. "Most days, I too felt like I was struggling for no apparent reason," says Sachar. The novel took him eighteen months to write, the exact length of Stanley's sentence at Camp Green Lake. Although it was a coincidence, Sachar says "maybe on some unconscious level, I knew how long it would take."

Sachar says he was influenced in his writing of *Holes* by Kurt Vonnegut's *Hocus Pocus* and William Goldman's *The Princess Bride*. "I like the way the opening chapters were sort of short and jumpy, and how they led into the story," Sachar says. "And *The Princess Bride* had these colorful characters and this bizarre setting, and that's sort of like *Holes*."[1]

The novel's structure was born of the need to tell separate stories from separate time periods. As he began the novel, for example, Sachar was concerned that the introduction of Elya Yelnats, Stanley's great-great-grandfather, would stop the progress of the plot. He also wondered how he could describe digging in an interesting way. "I wanted the reader to feel what a long, miserable experience this is, digging this five foot by five foot hole," Sachar says. "But how many times can you say, 'He dug his shovel back into the dirt and lifted out another shovelful'?"[1] He solved both problems by intertwining the stories, creating a rhythm that drives the reader through the story.

Of all his own novels, Sachar rates *Holes* as his favorite. "It was the greatest challenge to write," says Sachar, "and I feel like I met that challenge."

CRITICAL COMMENT

Sachar's struggle obviously paid off. *Holes* was the first book ever to win both the Newbery Medal and the National Book Award for Young People's Literature in the same year. Virginia McKee, committee chair for the Newbery Award, called the novel "masterfully unified in character, setting, and theme." Praise for *Holes* has been universal. Noting the "tightly fitted plot," and the "signifying wordplay," the *New York Times Book Review* described the novel as "a smart jigsaw puzzle of a novel that middle-grade youngsters will want to solve on their own."

[1]From "Louis Sachar: Top of His Class" by Barbara Strickland from *The Austin Chronicle Online*, accessed June 4, 2001, at http://www.auschron.com/issues/vol18/issue26/books.sachar.html.

Key Elements

Plot

Part One, Chapters 1–28 Stanley Yelnats and his family half-believe
that their bad luck is the result of the curse of a one-legged Gypsy
from whom Stanley's great-great-grandfather Elya stole a pig more
than a century ago in Latvia. The curse returns in the form of a pair
of smelly sneakers that hit Stanley on the head as he walks home
from a humiliating day at school. Everyone in his family believes that
Stanley stole the shoes of his hero, baseball star Clyde "Sweet Feet"
Livingston. The judge gives Stanley and his family a choice: jail or
Camp Green Lake. The camp turns out to be a juvenile detention
facility in the middle of a dried-up lake hours from civilization. The
boys are forced to dig holes in the lake bed, not knowing that they
are searching for buried treasure to enrich the Warden. For the first
time in his life, Stanley is accepted by his peers and even makes
friends. In exchange for help digging his holes, Stanley begins to
teach his new friend, Zero, to read.

Parts Two and Three, Chapters 29–50 A distant storm illuminates
a faraway mountain shaped like an enormous fist with its thumb
pointing to the sky. Stanley remembers that his great-grandfather—
the pig-stealer's son—who was robbed of his fortune by the outlaw
Kissin' Kate Barlow, survived in the desert by finding what he called
God's thumb. Could this be it? The next day, the other boys pick a
fight with Stanley because they are jealous of the help he is getting
from Zero. Zero smashes a shovel into a counselor's face and runs
away. A few days later, Stanley takes off after him. Zero is half dead
when Stanley finds him. They head slowly toward God's thumb,
hoping to find water, but halfway up the mountain, Zero collapses.
Now stronger from weeks of digging, Stanley is able to put Zero on
his shoulder and carry him the rest of the way. By carrying his friend
up the mountain, giving him water from the mountain, and singing
a certain Latvian lullaby, Stanley frees his family from the curse that
has been haunting it for generations. At the top of the mountain,
the boys survive on the water and onions they find there, and soon
they regain enough strength to return to the lake bed in search of
the treasure. They find it, but unfortunately the Warden finds them,
and the boys and the Warden end up in a standoff amid lethal
lizards until dawn, when the authorities rescue the boys and close
down the camp. The boys return to civilization to find that Stanley's
dad has finally invented something successful. Stanley's name is
cleared, Zero finds his mom, and the two boys get to split the con-
siderable booty.

Make a Connection

Ask students to remember a time when
they were falsely accused of a wrongdo-
ing. Invite them to describe their response
to the situation. How did they feel? How
was the situation resolved?

Structure and Point of View

There are two stories in *Holes:* the life of Stanley Yelnats at Camp Green Lake, and the fablelike tale of how Stanley's great-great-grandfather brings a curse down upon the family. Stanley Yelnats's story is told chronologically, interrupted with **flashbacks** that reveal the characters, settings, and actions in great-great-grandfather Yelnats's story. This story of intertwined generations is divided into three sections. In the first part, the story of Stanley and Camp Green Lake is set in motion, the background of the curse is given, and the sad history of the town of Green Lake and the drying up of the lake is revealed. The second part focuses on the turning point of Stanley's story—Zero and Stanley in the desert. Stanley saves Zero by using his knowledge of the Yelnats family's past and by doing so, he lifts the curse. The climax of the story is reached when Stanley and Zero discover the treasure in the lizards' nest and are confronted by the Warden. The brief third section is set almost a year and a half later and ties up the loose ends of both stories. The story is told from the **omniscient point of view,** allowing the reader to understand the thoughts and motivations of all the characters.

Major Themes

Courage in the face of adversity is shown when Stanley is subjected to harsh punishment at Camp Green Lake. Stanley comes to realize that he is strong, and his truly courageous spirit is revealed when he follows Zero into the desert.

The lives of others profoundly affect our own. Destinies intertwine and actions taken in one generation have an effect on those that follow.

The value of true friendship is realized by the previously friendless Stanley. Both he and Zero develop strong feelings of self-worth and caring for the other through helping one another.

Perseverance and optimism pay off. Even though Stanley and his family half-believe they are cursed, they do not let this belief stop them from working hard to succeed.

Characters

Students will meet the following **characters** in *Holes.*

Stanley Yelnats, at the beginning of the novel, is a friendless, overweight, middle-school student wrongly convicted of theft and sent to a desert correctional facility. Stanley is a **dynamic character**

Make a Connection

Ask students to describe briefly how the actions of their ancestors have affected their lives. These comments do not need to be shared.

Make a Connection

Ask students to think of the qualities they like most about their best friend or friends. Through class discussion, create a short list of these "friendly qualities."

Make a Connection

Ask students to remember a time when they succeeded in spite of difficulties. Discuss what students learned about optimism and perseverance through this experience.

whose moral and physical strength develop as he is forced to face his **internal conflict**—whether to help Zero or remain aloof—and his **external conflict**—surviving the camp itself.

Clyde "Sweet Feet" Livingston is a famous American League baseball player whose donated pair of sneakers sends Stanley to Camp Green Lake.

Stanley's family, and characters related to them, include:

Stanley Yelnats III, young Stanley's father, a failed inventor; **Elya Yelnats,** Stanley's no-good-dirty-rotten-pig-stealing great-great-grandfather from Latvia, who reputedly brought a curse on the family by forgetting a promise; **Madame Zeroni,** the wheelchair-bound Egyptian woman who gave Elya the secret to wooing his beloved and put a curse on the Yelnats family; **Myra Menke,** the pretty fourteen-year-old girl in Latvia whom Elya Yelnats wanted to marry; and **Igor Barkov,** the fifty-seven-year-old Latvian pig farmer who vies for—and wins—Myra's hand.

People who lived in the town of Green Lake over one hundred years ago include:

Miss Katherine Barlow, teacher in Green Lake who became **Kissin' Kate,** the outlaw, after the townspeople killed **Sam,** the African American onion seller, for kissing her. After Sam's murder, the lake dries up and the town dies. **Mary Lou** is Sam's onion-eating donkey.

Stanley Yelnats II is Stanley's great-grandfather, who lost his stock market fortune to Kissin' Kate and survived three weeks in the desert by finding the mountain he called God's thumb.

Charles "Trout" Walker is the rich, smelly Green Lake resident who loves Miss Katherine but hates learning. Rejected by Miss Katherine, he later marries another woman and becomes the Warden's father.

Sheriff is Kissin' Kate's first victim.

Camp Green Lake staff and inmates during Stanley's stay there include:

The Warden, the red-haired camp overseer whose main aim is to find the buried treasure; **Mr. Sir,** the irritable, gun-toting, cowboy-hat-wearing guard; **Mr. Pendanski** (Mom), the thoughtless and sometimes cruel camp counselor; **Squid** (Alan), who threatens to pound Stanley if he reveals Squid's nighttime crying; **X-Ray** (pig Latin for Rex), the near-blind bully and leader of the group; **Magnet** (José), named for his thievery; **Armpit** (Theodore), the second-biggest camp inmate after Stanley; and **Zigzag** (Ricky) who has frizzy blond hair and a long skinny neck topped by a big round head. **Zero** (Hector Zeroni), uneducated but smart, becomes Stanley's friend. Coincidentally, he is a descendant of Madame Zeroni, the Egyptian woman who put a curse on the Yelnats family in Latvia. **Twitch** (Brian) is the car thief who takes Zero's place in camp after Zero runs away.

Last, but not least:

Ms. Morengo, Stanley's father's patent attorney, rescues Stanley and Zero. She is accompanied by the **Attorney General,** the chief law enforcement officer in Texas.

Setting

Although part of the story is set in Latvia, Camp Green Lake is the main setting of the novel. Sachar describes its prosperity and lush beauty of more than a century ago, when Green Lake supported a thriving town and was surrounded by bountiful peach trees. The author creates a distinctly different atmosphere by describing the dry lake bed and parched landscape where the current action unfolds. The harsh climate is an important element in the story.

Literary Elements

Throughout the novel, Sachar uses **irony** for humor or to make a point, as with the name of the camp. However, for some aspects of the story, the reader will not fully understand the discrepancy between what is expected and what actually happens until the end of the novel. Sachar enlivens his narrative with **sensory descriptions** as well as with **figures of speech,** such as **similes** ("It was as if they had been walking across the flat bottom of a giant frying pan, and now they had to somehow climb up out of it.") and **metaphors** ("The horizon lit up with a huge web of lightning.").

Make a Connection

Have students find out how the place where they live has changed over the last hundred years. Discuss how these changes reflect events that occurred over the years.

Before You Read

Options

Engaging Issues

The issues raised in Holes *continue to be relevant and controversial today. This activity encourages students to grapple with these issues in ways relevant to their own lives.*

Use the following list to introduce the issues. Have students read each item on the list, tell what they think that word means to them, and then prepare a brief response explaining why they feel this way. The response should contain at least one concrete example from their knowledge or experience.

When students are finished, they can gather in small groups to discuss their responses and attempt to reach a consensus. Alternatively, have students use the list and responses for a class discussion.

List:

- Friendship
- Courage
- Punishment
- Failure
- Outlaw
- Prejudice
- Perseverance
- Bullying

ROLE-PLAYING

Falsely Accused

Team up with another student and role-play a discussion between a judge and someone your age who is falsely accused of a crime. After one student has taken the role of the innocent victim and the other the judge, switch roles and repeat the exercise. Then, discuss which is more difficult: being a teenager accused of something you did not do, or an adult who has to decide if you are telling the truth. As you read, look for a similar type of confrontation in *Holes*.

RESEARCH

It's Hot Out There

Much of *Holes* is set in a hot, barren area of Texas. This setting becomes a major obstacle for Stanley as he tries to survive at Camp Green Lake. To help you imagine what it might be like to live in such a place, research a similar environment using the Web and resources in the library. Select one aspect of an environment—the temperature, scarcity of water, or the reptiles and other animals that live there—and prepare a short presentation for the class.

MAKING PERSONAL CONNECTIONS

My Friend

In your journal, write about your idea of what a friend should be. List the qualities you most admire in a friend. As you will not need to share this writing, go on to tell about two or three of your closest friends. What attracted you to these people? What do you and your friends do together? Do you tell your friends your secrets? Why or why not? Do you have a best friend? Who is it, and why? Make a list of the ways you think a friendship grows.

MAKING PREDICTIONS

And Then What?

In a group of three or four classmates, listen carefully as one member reads aloud chapters 1 and 2. Then, as a group, discuss what you think the story is about. What do you think will happen to Stanley Yelnats? What do you think the camp will be like? Record your group's predictions on a piece of paper. During a whole-class discussion, present your predictions and see how they compare to those of other groups. Consult your list as you read the novel.

Glossary and Vocabulary

- **Vocabulary Words** are preceded by an asterisk (*) and may appear in the Vocabulary Worksheets.
- Words are listed in their order of appearance.
- The definition and the part of speech are based on the way the word is used in the chapter. For other uses of the word, check a dictionary.

Part One

hammock *n.:* strip of heavy cloth or netting suspended between two trees or posts and used for sleeping or lounging

*****stifling** *adj.:* suffocating; so stuffy and warm as to make one feel smothered

*****descendants** *n.:* offspring; people who are the children, grandchildren, great-grandchildren, and so on, of a certain person or group

*****gruff** *adj.:* rough or hoarse

*****perseverance** *n.:* persistence; continued effort

*****barren** *adj.:* without plant life; empty

*****desolate** *adj.:* deserted; ruined and abandoned

*****wearily** *adv.:* in an extremely tired way

*****prospect** *n.:* hopeful anticipation; an expectation

*****mere** *adj.:* simple; only; no more than

*****destiny** *n.:* what must certainly happen; fate

*****despicable** *adj.:* deserving to be looked down on or hated

*****defective** *adj.:* faulty; lacking an important or necessary quality

*****forlorn** *adj.:* without hope; miserable

*****deftly** *adv.:* in a quick and skillful way

*****reluctantly** *adv.:* in an unwilling way

*****preposterous** *adj.:* ridiculous; so absurd as to be laughable

*****dawdle** *v.:* to waste time; to be idle

*****aimlessly** *adv.:* without a goal, purpose, or direction

wharf *n.:* a platform or dock built at the edge of a body of water for boats or ships to use during loading and unloading

pier *n.:* a structure built out over the water and used as a landing place for boats or ships

*****enviously** *v.:* in a jealous way

*****predatory** *adj.:* catching and eating other animals

*****scowled** *v.:* looked angry or threatening

*****smug** *adj.:* conceited or self-satisfied; overly contented with oneself

*****paranoid** *adj.:* extremely suspicious or mistrustful, especially without reason

*****presumably** *adv.:* probably

*****evict** *v.:* to remove by legal order a tenant from a rented house or property, especially for nonpayment of rent or for causing disturbances

*****penetrating** *adj.:* keen; searching

burlap *n.:* a type of coarse cloth used in sacks

concoctions *n.:* compounds made up of a combination of ingredients

Parts Two and Three

*recede *v.:* to decrease; to lessen

*writhed *v.:* twisted or squirmed, as in great pain

*defiance *n.:* resistance against or challenge to authority

*astonishment *n.:* surprise; amazement

*grotesque *adj.:* extremely distorted in appearance

*parched *adj.:* hot and dry; shriveled

*quivering *adj.:* shaking; trembling

"Forty days and forty nights . . .": a reference to the Biblical story of Noah and the Flood (Genesis 7), in which God told Noah and his family to take two of each animal onto an ark (a boat) to ride out the forty days and forty nights of rain that would destroy the rest of the world

*delirious *adj.:* raving; in a state of wild excitement or emotion, especially as with a high fever or certain types of mental illness

*feeble *adj.:* extremely weak; not effective

*altitude *n.:* height above a base level such as the earth's surface

*increments *n.:* additions; small amounts of increase

*precipice *n.:* a steep rock or cliff

*contritely *adv.:* apologetically; humbly regretful

sundial *n.:* a device that measures time by the shadow cast by a pin or post on a dial marked with hours

*inexplicable *adj.:* not explainable or easily understood

*distinctive *adj.:* easily recognizable; particular; characteristic of one thing or person as opposed to others

*precarious *adj.:* unstable; dangerous

*commotion *n.:* violent activity or disturbance

*rigid *adj.:* not moving or bending

*strenuous *adj.:* difficult; tiring

hallucinations *n.:* illusions of seeing or hearing sights or sounds that are not in fact present

detainees *n.:* persons being held in confinement, as in a jail

jurisdiction *n.:* legal authority or control

pursuant *adj.:* following; because of

patent attorney *n.:* a lawyer who assists inventors in protecting their ideas and products from being copied or sold by others

*tedious *adj.:* boring

stock certificates *n.:* documents that provide evidence of ownership of shares in a particular company

deeds of trust *n.:* documents that transfer, from one person or group to another, a certain share in a property

promissory notes *n.:* IOUs; written promises to pay a particular sum of money to a particular person on a particular date

First Thoughts

1. What do you think about Stanley's response to Camp Green Lake? How would you feel in his place?

Shaping Interpretations

2. Sometimes an author uses the **setting** of a novel to create **conflict** for a character. How does the parched lake bed in *Holes* become an obstacle that Stanley must overcome?

3. Why did Madame Zeroni tell Stanley's great-great grandfather, Elya Yelnats, to carry a piglet up a mountain every day for two months so it could drink from a stream?

4. An author sometimes uses **sensory descriptions,** or details that appeal to one of the reader's five senses, to make a narrative more interesting. In *Holes,* how does Sachar use the sense of smell?

5. **Irony** is the contrast between expectation and reality. How is the name of Camp Green Lake ironic? Why is Zero's name ironic?

6. Why do you think the author uses nicknames for so many of his characters?

7. Sachar uses **flashbacks** to introduce events that happened at an earlier time. Give one example in which the author interrupts the action of the plot in this manner.

READING CHECK

a. What is Camp Green Lake?

b. What are Stanley and all the boys at Camp Green Lake forced to do?

c. Why does Stanley's family always blame their bad luck on Stanley's great-great-grandfather?

d. Stanley does not tell his mother the truth about the camp in his letters home. Why?

e. How does Zero persuade Stanley to teach him to read?

f. Why did Miss Katherine, Green Lake's teacher, become Kissin' Kate Barlow, the notorious outlaw?

Connecting with the Text

8. At school Stanley has no friends, but at the camp, he is accepted by the other boys and that surprises and pleases him. Have you ever been treated a certain way by one group of peers, and a completely different way by another group? How did you feel?

Extending the Text

9. Stanley is severely punished for a crime he did not commit. Discuss an example of this kind of unfair treatment from your own experience, or from your reading, television programs or movie viewing.

Challenging the Text

10. The boys in the camp do not think it is fair that Zero is helping to dig Stanley's holes. What do you think of Stanley's decision to trade teaching Zero to read for Zero's work at digging holes?

Reading Strategies: Part One

Part One, Summarizing

Louis Sachar tells several stories in *Holes.* One is Stanley's story, set in the present time. Stanley's story is interrupted by Elya Yelnats's and Kissin' Kate's stories. These stories use flashbacks to tell the history of Stanley's family. These stories are not told in chronological, or time, order.

In the boxes below, briefly retell each character's story chronologically.

Elya Yelnats's Story

Kissin' Kate Barlow's Story

Stanley Yelnats's Story

FOLLOW-UP: Based on these stories, predict what you think will happen to Stanley in the next part of the novel.

_____

_____

_____

_____

Novel Notes

LATVIA
★Riga

Part One, *Holes*

The Word PLACE

What's in a Name?

Nickname came from the Old Norse word *eke-name. Eke* meant "a piece added on." Do you have a nickname? What is it?

Where in the World?

Latvia, formerly part of the Soviet Union, became an independent country in 1991. Only slightly larger than West Virginia, it is basically a rolling plain, with two thirds covered with forests, swamps, pastures, and wasteland. Manufacturing is the main source of income in Latvia; the heavy machine building industry produces radios, refrigerators, washing machines, and motor scooters.

FOR YOUR READER'S LOG

How would it feel to be homeless?

Motor Scooter

History in a Nutshell: *Gunslingers*

The Wild West had many famous gunslingers, but few were women. Two famous female outlaws were Belle Starr and Calamity Jane.

"Belle"—Myra Bell Shirley—dressed as a "bandit queen" in "velvet and feathers or buckskin and moccasins." She married several outlaws, developing a reputation for helping criminals. Her unsolved murder added to the mystery of her life. "Calamity Jane"—Martha Jane Cannary—was allegedly associated with another outlaw, Wild Bill Hickok, and was buried beside him in Deadwood, South Dakota.

Martha Jane Cannary

Medicine Cabinet I

Everyone's had a blister, but what is it? A blister forms when heat caused by friction, a burn, a sting, or a virus builds up between the epidermis (outer skin) and dermis (deeper layer of skin with nerves and blood vessels). You are probably most familiar with friction blisters that can be caused by new shoes or manual labor—repeated rubbing on the same patch of skin, causing a buildup of fluid. The best treatment for a blister is to leave it alone. If it is uncomfortable, a blister can be drained by opening the skin with a sterilized needle; it should then be covered with a clean bandage.

Quotation Corner

*"Let onion atoms lurk within the bowl
And, scarce suspected, animate the whole."*

Sydney Smith
Recipe for salad
Lady Holland's Memoir
[1855]

Choices: Part One

Building Your Portfolio

CREATIVE WRITING

More Sincerely Yours

In his letters home, Stanley makes up stories about what he does at Camp Green Lake. Rewrite Stanley's two letters, describing how Camp Green Lake really is. Be sure to describe the setting, tell what has happened so far, and include details about at least two of the characters at the camp. When you finish, exchange your letters with a classmate. Discuss how your letters are alike and how they are different.

ART

Picture This

The hot, desolate setting of *Holes* plays an important part in the novel. Based on what you have read so far, draw or paint a picture of the setting. You can use details from the novel to make your representation look realistic, or you can interpret the setting abstractly, using only colors and shapes to give a feeling of the isolated, parched camp. Display your finished work with other students' pictures, and with the class, discuss the different interpretations of the setting that the novel has inspired.

COLLECTION

Pack Your Bags

With two or three other classmates, make a list of the six most necessary items to take with you if you had to go to Camp Green Lake. Make sure all of the items would fit into Stanley's backpack. Number the items in importance, and display them for the rest of the class. Include a card that explains why each item is necessary.

RESEARCH

Lizards and Scorpions and Rattlin' Snakes

Select one of the creatures that inhabit the desert at Camp Green Lake and find out about it. Where does it live? What does it eat? What is the most interesting fact about the creature you selected? Organize your results and display them on a chart for the class. Be sure to include some type of illustration.

Consider This . . .

"I want you to know, Stanley, that I respect you," Mr. Pendanski said. "I understand you've made some bad mistakes in your life. Otherwise you wouldn't be here. But everyone makes mistakes. You may have done some bad things, but that doesn't mean you're a bad kid."

Based on what Mr. Pendanski says, how does he feel about Stanley and the other boys? Describe how his later actions support or do not support his statement.

Writing Follow-up: Compare and Contrast _____ ■

The judge gives Stanley two options: jail or Camp Green Lake. Do you agree with Stanley's choice? In two to four paragraphs, defend or disagree with Stanley's decision. Offer at least two reasons for your position, and support each reason with examples or facts.

Novel Notes

Create an activity based on **Novel Notes, Issue 1.** Here are two suggestions.

- Find out about any of your relatives who came from another country.
- Find out what the punishment would be in your community for stealing a pair of sneakers valued at $5,000.

Making Meanings: Parts Two and Three

First Thoughts

1. Why do you think things suddenly worked out for Stanley and his family?

Shaping Interpretations

2. How are Stanley and Zero different? How are they alike?

3. At the beginning of Part Two, how does the author use **foreshadowing** to hint that events are speeding up and things are about to change?

4. When Zero runs away, the Warden destroys all of Zero's files so that when he dies in the desert, no one will come looking for him. What outcome makes this act an example of **irony**?

5. Why do you think Stanley follows Zero into the desert?

READING CHECK

a. What does Zero do after the big fight on Zigzag's birthday?

b. What is the Warden's real reason for making the boys dig holes in the lake bed?

c. How does Stanley finally respond to Zero's departure?

d. What helps Zero survive in the desert, but eventually makes him sick to his stomach?

e. How do Zero and Stanley regain enough strength to return to camp?

f. What was the buried treasure that Stanley and Zero discovered?

6. Summarize what happens to the boys from the time that Stanley discovers Zero under the boat until the Warden finds the boys with the treasure.

7. At the **climax,** or moment of greatest suspense of the novel, how do Stanley and Zero escape the Warden, Mr. Sir, Mr. Pendanski, and the lethal yellow-spotted lizards?

Connecting with the Text

8. Stanley discovers many connections and similarities between his own life and the lives of his great-grandfather and his great-great-grandfather. Have you ever uncovered a connection or similarity between you and another family member that surprised you? Explain your answer and give an example.

Extending the Text

9. Stanley and Hector Zeroni overcome many of their difficulties by helping each other. Do you think this is the basis for a good friendship? Explain your answer, giving examples from your own experience, or from your reading.

Challenging the Text

10. In the end, everyone in the story gets what he or she deserves. Do you agree with the way Sachar ends the novel, or do you think it should have ended differently? Explain your answer.

Reading Strategies: Parts Two and Three

Holes

Parts Two and Three: Drawing Conclusions

Stanley chooses to follow Zero into the desert and try to save him.

On each side of the scale below, write three considerations Stanley had to think about before he made his decision. One has been done for you.

Stay and Wait

Zero might come back

Follow Zero

FOLLOW-UP: Given the considerations you have listed, would you have made the same decision as Stanley? Explain your answer.

_____

_____

_____

Parts Two and Three, *Holes*

Medicine Cabinet II
This food is *killing* me!

Canned food that has been improperly sterilized contains a toxin, or poison, that can cause paralysis—even death! Do not eat canned food if

• the food smells unpleasant;

• the lid bulges, leaks, or looks corroded;

• the coloring is unnatural;

• the liquid is cloudy; or

• you can see mold.

The Perfect Storm–Estimating Method

Do not let a thunderstorm take you by surprise. Estimate how far away you are from a thunderstorm by counting the seconds—one thousand one, one thousand two, one thousand three, and so on—between a flash of lightning and the following thunderclap. Then, divide this number by five to get the distance in miles. If you can hear thunder, you could be a target for lightning—a thunderstorm does not have to be overhead to be dangerous.

Who's Mother Goose?

Legend has it that she was Elizabeth Goose from Boston, whose grave is a tourist attraction, but no evidence has been found of the rhymes she supposedly wrote in 1719. A collection of early nursery rhymes called *Mother Goose's Melody; or Sonnets for the Cradle,* was published in 1781 in England. The name "Mother Goose" may have come from a French folk expression for "old wives' tales." The nursery rhyme that Zero did

not recognize is usually part of a Mother Goose collection, and it goes like this:

> There was an old woman who lived in a shoe,
> She had so many children she didn't know what to do;

> She gave them some broth without any bread,
> Then whipped them all soundly and put them to bed.

What's Cookin?

"Spiced" peaches are seasoned with cloves, white and brown sugar, and cinnamon.

INVESTIGATE • *How do animals find water in the desert?*

Name _____ Date _____

Choices: Parts Two and Three

Building Your Portfolio

ART
A Big Thumbs-Up

Using air-drying clay or papier-mâché, create a sculpture of the mountain where Stanley and Zero find refuge. Be sure to consult the novel for details. Include the boys, the onions, and their "watering hole" in your sculpture. Display your work with other students' work in the classroom. Did everyone have the same idea of what the mountain looked like?

READER'S THEATER
And . . . Action!

With a small group of classmates, choose an exciting scene from Part Two or Part Three of the novel. Then, write a script for the scene. Use dialogue directly from the book, and add any other spoken lines that you think are necessary for clarity and interest. Using simple props and costumes, rehearse the scene with your classmates. Then, perform it for the class. Ask another classmate to videotape your performance so you can review it later.

CREATIVE WRITING
The Song of Stanley

Stanley knows one verse of the Latvian lullaby that began with Madame Zeroni. At the end of the novel, Zero's mother sings another verse. Write your own verse for this ancient but imaginary song. Include the same sort of imagery, like the moon and the wolf, so that your verse fits with the other two. Then, sing or recite your verse to the class.

Consider This . . .
Stanley was surprised that he himself hadn't gotten sick—either from the Sploosh, the dirty water, or from living on onions. He used to get sick quite a lot back home.

What do Stanley's thoughts tell you about how he has changed since he left home?

Writing Follow-up: Cause and Effect

In two to four paragraphs, explore the causes and effects suggested by the above quote. Offer at least two causes for why Stanley used to get sick. Then, discuss at least two causes for Stanley's newfound health and strength. What effect might his new physical fitness have when Stanley returns to his old school?

Novel Notes

Create an activity based on **Novel Notes, Issue 2.** Here are two suggestions.

- Find out about the origin of another nursery rhyme.
- Find out how people can find water and food in the desert.

Writing About the Novel

Copyright © by Holt, Rinehart and Winston. All rights reserved.

SHORT STORY
The Z Files

In Part Three of the novel, it becomes clear that Hector Zeroni has finally found his mother. However, the author does not say how he found her or what happens to them later. Write a short story that tells about Hector and his mother after the novel ends. Create a literary magazine by grouping your story with stories written by other classmates. Publish the magazine by distributing copies to your class.
(Creative Writing)

PRESENTING AN OPINION
Is It a "Must Read"?

Many reviewers have lavished praise on *Holes* but you may not agree with their viewpoints. Write a review in which you offer your own opinion of the novel. Use details from the novel to back up your opinions. Then, pair up with a student whose view opposes your own, and present your reviews to the class.
(Critical Writing)

LEGEND
Once Upon a Time

According to family legend, Stanley's great-great-grandfather was cursed by a one-legged Egyptian in Latvia. When times get tough, they half-jokingly blame the curse for the family's repeated misfortune. Write your own legend about your family. Illustrate your tale with your own drawings or with pictures you cut out of magazines or photocopy from other publications.
(Creative Writing)

PERSUADING WITH AN EDITORIAL
And Justice For All

The authorities at Camp Green Lake believe that digging holes in the hot sun turns a bad boy into a good boy. Is this the way reform really works? Research the juvenile justice system in your state. Then, write an editorial about where it succeeds and how it fails. Be sure to explain how the system works, give your opinion about it, then offer a way to make the system better.
(Critical Writing)

SHAGGY DOG STORY
There once was a . . .

Several critics have commented that *Holes* is a type of shaggy dog story. Find out exactly what kind of story this is—hint: consult the dictionary, use the library and the Web. Then, outline your own shaggy dog story and write it. Present your story to the class as an oral reading.
(Creative Writing)

Cross-Curricular Connections

GEOLOGY

Fossil Record

Not only was Camp Green Lake once underwater—almost all of Texas was at one time covered by an ocean. How do geologists know this? Fossils tell the story. Create a geological time line for Texas showing the state from prehistoric times until now. Include representations of fossils to illustrate what creatures lived at the bottom of the sea during each period on your time line.

SCIENCE

Ingenious Inventions

Stanley's father is an inventor who at last finds success with his antidote to foot odor in sneakers. Research an actual inventor from the past, and organize your results in the form of a chart with illustrations. Include information about the life of the inventor, and about at least one important invention that he or she created. Be sure to include a drawing or photo of the invention, or create a working model. Give a history of the invention—how it worked, its importance, how it influenced other inventors, and whether or not it is still in use. Present the results of your research to the class.

GEOGRAPHY

It's Like a Whole Other Country

Texas gets even hotter than the 95-degree days Sachar describes in his novel. And while part of the state is a desert, Texas supports many different ecosystems. Create a three-dimensional topographical map of the state that shows these different areas. Include mountains, the major rivers, and the locations of the five largest cities. Display your model to the class and discuss how Sachar's novel would be different if he had set it in another part of the state, such as East Texas.

HOME ECONOMICS

It's Peaches!

How many different ways can you use peaches to create a mouth watering dish? Make a collection of recipes that use either fresh or canned peaches. Collate them into a booklet and illustrate it. Choose one of the recipes or create your own and prepare a peachy dish for the class to sample. Demonstrate how to prepare your peach recipe, or prepare a series of slides or posters that show how to prepare it. Present your collation to the class.

Multimedia and Internet Connections

NOTE: Check with your teacher about school policies on accessing Internet sites.

SOUNDTRACK

You Write the Songs

Some movie soundtracks are so good they stand as successful albums on their own, and you do not have to watch the movie to enjoy the music over and over again. Many of these albums have no words. Rather, they create a feeling through sound alone. Imagine that a famous director is making a movie of *Holes* and wants you to create the soundtrack. Try to capture the mood of the setting in your soundtrack. Do not be limited by traditional instruments. Incorporate sounds from nature—screeching cicadas, bird cries, wind blowing across sand. Some musicians even bang on trash cans or brake drums to get the right sound. When you have finished, play your soundtrack to the class.

INTERNET RESEARCH & WEB DESIGN

Living La Vida Latvia

Stanley's no-good-dirty-rotten-great-great-grandfather was from Latvia. Research Latvia in reference resources and on the Web. As well as the history of the country, be sure to check out tourism and travel sites. Then, create a Web page to lure tourists to Latvia. Include pictures you have found or created as well as text you have written. Keep the tone light and appealing so viewers will want to visit the areas you describe.

NEWSPAPER REPORTING

Extra! Extra! Write All About It!

The Attorney General's office has shut down Camp Green Lake. That's big news in the area; in fact, it's the only news in the area. Break into groups of six or seven students, and publish your own special edition of the *Green Lake Express-News.* Study your hometown newspaper and at least one national newspaper to see how the professionals do it. You'll need at least two reporters to write the stories; one editorial writer to write an opinion piece; one photographer to take the pictures; one cartoonist to draw the editorial cartoon; and one layout artist to put the package all together. Other potential positions include a graphic artist to draw maps and charts, a feature writer to put together a background piece, or an editor to make sure everything is well written and accurate.

VIDEO PERFORMANCE

Caught in the Act

There were rumors at Camp Green Lake that the Warden had video cameras hidden in several locations so she could always keep an eye on the inmates. With one or two other classmates, write a script for a scene that could have been captured by one of those hidden cameras. Then, using simple props and costumes, act out the script and record your performance on videotape. Remember that your camera is supposed to be hidden, so be sure your footage corresponds to the point of view of the hidden camera. Show the video to your classmates. Do they agree the scene you filmed could actually have happened in the book?

Name _____ Date _____

Reading Skills and Strategies Worksheet

Novel Organizer

Holes

CHARACTER

Use the chart below to keep track of the characters in this novel. Each time you come across a new character, write the character's name and the number of the page on which the character first appears. Then, jot down a brief description. Add information about the characters as you read. Put a star next to the name of each main character.

NAME OF CHARACTER	PAGE	DESCRIPTION

Reading Skills and Strategies Worksheet *(cont.)*

Novel Organizer *(continued)*   *Holes*

SETTING

Where and when does this story take place? ....

....

....

CONFLICT (Read at least seven chapters before you answer.)

What is the biggest problem faced by the main character(s)? ....

....

....

How do you predict it will be resolved? ....

....

....

MAJOR EVENTS

- ....

- ....

- ....

- ....

- ....

OUTCOME

How is the main problem resolved? (How accurate was your prediction?) ....

....

....

Literary Elements Worksheet 1

Theme

A **theme** is an insight about human life that an author develops in a work of fiction. In *Holes*, Stanley discovers how other people's actions profoundly affect his own life.

How do the actions of each of these characters affect Stanley? Trout Walker has been done for you.

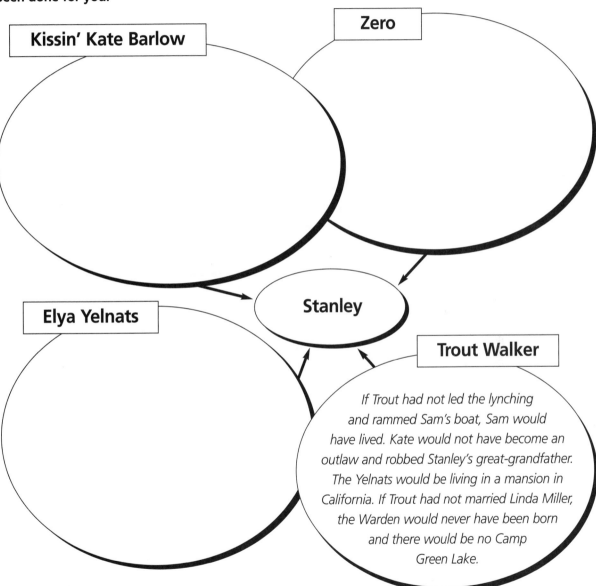

FOLLOW-UP: When Zero runs away, the Warden orders all of his files destroyed. What is the unintended consequence of this action?

_____

_____

_____

Literary Elements Worksheet 2

Irony

Irony relies on the contrast between what is expected and what really happens. Often in *Holes,* Sachar will introduce a statement, and the reader does not realize it is ironic until much later in the novel.

In the boxes below, describe how the following statements are ironic. One has been done for you.

1. "This isn't a Girl Scout camp," said Mr. Sir.

is ironic because

2. "I'm not going to run away," Stanley said.

"Good thinking," said Mr. Sir. "Nobody runs away from here."

is ironic because

Not only does Stanley end up running away, so does Zero. They both succeed in getting away.

3. "I want you to know, Stanley, that I respect you," Mr. Pendanski said.

is ironic because

4. "Clyde Livingston testified that they were his sneakers and that he had donated them to help raise money for the homeless shelter. He said he couldn't imagine what kind of horrible person would steal from homeless children."

is ironic because

FOLLOW-UP: Sachar also uses irony when he names people and places. How are the names of Clyde "Sweet Feet" Livingston and X-Ray ironic?

_____

_____

_____

_____

Literary Elements Worksheet 3

Holes

Figures of Speech: Metaphors and Similes

A simile is a figure of speech that makes a comparison between two unlike things using words such as *like, as, than,* and *resembles.* A metaphor makes a comparison by stating that one thing is another, such as "nerves of steel."

For each quotation below, record what two things are being compared and tell whether the figure of speech is a metaphor or a simile. One has been done for you.

Quotation	Things Being Compared	Metaphor? Simile?
1. "He's a mole," Zigzag had said.		
2. "His real name is Charles Walker, but everyone called him Trout because his two feet smelled like a couple of dead fish."		
3. "Zero's face looked like a jack-o'-lantern that had been left out too many days past Halloween—half rotten, with sunken eyes and a drooping smile."		
4. The horizon lit up with a huge web of lightning.	*horizon and web*	*metaphor*
5. "Oh, Sam," she said. "My heart is breaking."		

FOLLOW-UP: On the lines below, record a metaphor or simile from the book that is not included above.

_____

_____

_____

Vocabulary Worksheet 1   **Part One**

Holes

A. Circle the letter of the word or phrase that most nearly defines the italicized word in each excerpt from *Holes*.

1. Supposedly, he had a great-grandfather who had stolen a pig from a one-legged Gypsy, and she put a curse on him and all his *descendants.*
   a. offspring   **b.** livestock   **c.** friends   **d.** neighbors

2. In his mind he could hear his father's *gruff* voice softly singing to him.
   a. high   **b.** deep   **c.** hoarse   **d.** sweet

3. To be a successful inventor you need three things: intelligence, *perseverance,* and just a little bit of luck.
   a. fussiness   **b.** persistence   **c.** information   **d.** superiority

4. The boys glanced *wearily* at Stanley.
   a. in a laughing way   **b.** sadly   **c.** quickly   **d.** in a tired way

5. It was too much of a coincidence to be a *mere* accident.
   a. dangerous   **b.** casual   **c.** simple   **d.** lucky

6. The judge called Stanley's crime *despicable.*
   a. hateful   **b.** harmless   **c.** suspicious   **d.** peculiar

7. He glanced helplessly at his shovel. It wasn't *defective.* He was defective.
   a. strong   **b.** powerless   **c.** faulty   **d.** dependent

8. Madame Zeroni hated to see Elya so *forlorn.*
   a. hungry   **b.** careless   **c.** confused   **d.** miserable

9. He popped some sunflower seeds into his mouth, *deftly* removed the shells with his teeth, and spat them into Stanley's hole.
   a. noisily   **b.** skillfully   **c.** rudely   **d.** slowly

10. *Reluctantly,* he climbed up out of his hole, and once again dug his shovel into his previously dug dirt.
   a. unwillingly   **b.** nervously   **c.** proudly   **d.** uncertainly

11. "That's *preposterous!*" exclaimed Igor, expelling saliva as he spoke.
   a. interesting   **b.** ridiculous   **c.** sensible   **d.** precious

12. Stanley took a long, deep breath. He couldn't afford to *dawdle.*
  a. spend money   **b.** be silly   **c.** waste time   **d.** be angry

13. "You're finished?" Stanley asked *enviously.*
  a. politely   **b.** calmly   **c.** jealously   **d.** sneeringly

14. "Just what do you think you're doing?" asks Squid, as he slams his hands into Derrick Dunne's *smug* face.
  a. ugly   **b.** handsome   **c.** unguarded   **d.** conceited

15. Zero stared at him with *penetrating* eyes.
  a. calm   **b.** piercing   **c.** dark   **d.** sleepy

B. Read carefully the definition of each word. Then, write a sentence of your own using that word. If possible, include in your sentences clues to the meanings of the defined words.

16. stifling, *adj.:* suffocating; so stuffy and warm as to make one feel smothered

_____

_____

17. desolate, *adj.:* deserted; ruined and abandoned

_____

_____

18. aimlessly, *adv.:* without a goal, purpose, or direction

_____

_____

19. scowled, *v.:* looked angry or threatening

_____

_____

20. presumably, *adv.:* probably

_____

_____

Name _____ Date _____

Vocabulary Worksheet 2 Parts Two and Three

A. Circle the letter of the word or phrase that most nearly defines the italicized word in each excerpt from *Holes*.

1. For a second, Mr. Sir's pain seemed to *recede*.

   a. worsen   **b.** lessen   **c.** be imaginary   **d.** be unbearable

2. For a second, he thought he saw a flash of *defiance* in Zero's eyes, but then it passed.

   a. challenge   **b.** understanding   **c.** worry   **d.** obedience

3. He felt a jolt of *astonishment*.

   a. electricity   **b.** recognition   **c.** amazement   **d.** acceptance

4. No one said anything except "Thank you, Mr. Sir" as he filled each canteen. No one even dared to look at his *grotesque* face.

   a. grinning   **b.** sunburned   **c.** distorted   **d.** cruel

5. They didn't see her, but she saw them. She pointed her *quivering* finger in their direction and whispered, "God will punish you!"

   a. accusing   **b.** disapproving   **c.** stiff   **d.** shaking

6. No one ever knew what he meant by that. He was *delirious* when he said it.

   a. clever   **b.** raving   **c.** mysterious   **d.** whispering

7. Stanley made a *feeble* attempt to punch Zigzag, then he felt a flurry of fists against his head and neck.

   a. weak   **b.** furious   **c.** sudden   **d.** comical

8. Instead they zigzagged back and forth, increasing their *altitude* by small increments every time they changed directions.

   a. weakness   **b.** cheerfulness   **c.** height   **d.** strength

9. He took a deep breath, then walked the last fifty yards to the giant *precipice* and touched it.

   a. monument   **b.** cliff   **c.** tree   **d.** crater

10. "I'm glad Becca's all right," Hattie said *contritely*.

   a. respectfully   **b.** courageously   **c.** shyly   **d.** apologetically

11. As they got closer he occasionally could hear Mr. Sir's *distinctive* bark.

   a. unusually loud   **b.** obviously mad   **c.** easily recognizable   **d.** deep-voiced

Vocabulary Worksheet 2 *(cont.)*   **Parts Two and Three**

Holes

12. As his tunnel grew deeper and wider—and more *precarious*—Stanley was able to feel latches on one end of the box, and then a leather handle.

    a. unstable   **b.** sheltered   **c.** roomy   **d.** organized

13. His legs were sore from remaining *rigid* for so long.

    a. in motion   **b.** stiff   **c.** bent   **d.** crossed

14. Standing still was more *strenuous* than walking.

    a. satisfying   **b.** energizing   **c.** restful   **d.** tiring

15. The reader probably still has some questions, but unfortunately, from here on in, the answers tend to be long and *tedious.*

    a. complicated   **b.** drawn out   **c.** boring   **d.** troubling

B. **Read carefully the definition of each word. Then, write a sentence of your own using that word. If possible, include in your sentences clues to the meanings of the defined words.**

16. writhed, *v.:* twisted or squirmed, as in great pain

_____

_____

17. parched, *adj.:* hot and dry; shriveled

_____

_____

18. increments, *n.:* additions; small amounts of increase

_____

_____

19. inexplicable, *adj.:* not explainable or easily understood

_____

_____

20. commotion, *n.:* violent activity or disturbance

_____

_____

Introducing the Connections

The **Connections** that follow this novel in the HRW LIBRARY edition create the opportunity for students to relate the book's themes to other genres, times, and places and to their own lives. The following chart will facilitate your use of these additional works. Succeeding pages offer **Making Meanings** questions to stimulate student response.

Selection	Summary, Connection to Novel
About the Onion *nonfiction Web article*	Onions are not only vegetables that add zest to many dishes, they also have an interesting history. In *Holes,* the onion lives up to its reputation and plays a major role in saving the lives of Stanley and Zero.
The Girl Who Loved the Sky Anita Endrezze *poem*	The story of a friendship and the resulting feeling of bitterness that comes when that friendship is lost is the subject of this poem by a Yaqui poet. Stanley's story is the reverse—he goes from bitter loneliness to the joy of friendship with Zero.
What are Palindromes? *nonfiction Web article*	Palindromes have been around for a long time and are a fascinating way to play with letters and words. The Yelnats family has used this device for generations.
Ethan Explains the B and B Inn from *The View from Saturday* E. L. Konigsburg *novel excerpt*	Ethan Potter is a loner—he is the longest rider on the bus and tries very hard to make sure that he is the only person in his seat. Then, a new boy arrives in town, and what a sight he is in his knee socks and shorts. No one in Epiphany wears knee socks and shorts. This is a tale of a friendship that releases Ethan from his loneliness, just as Stanley's friendship with Zero gave both of them a new life.

Introducing the Connections

Selection	Summary, Connection to Novel
Modern Science Takes a Look at an Ancient Monster Bert Gildart *magazine article*	Although the Gila monster can be painfully poisonous, it seems to reserve its venom for times when it needs protection. How did scientists find this out? This article tells how researchers are discovering the secrets of this creature that has been roaming our deserts since prehistoric times. The Gila monster could have provided a model for the dreadfully poisonous lizards in *Holes*.
The Snake King retold by Kathleen Arnott *folk tale*	Temba enters the kingdom of the Snake King and by doing so, finds that he must undergo a trial to prove his friendship with the magical King. Symbolic elements in this folk tale mirror those in *Holes*, as do the lessons learned by both Temba and Stanley.

Exploring the Connections

Making Meanings

About the Onion

1. Why was the fact that onions did not spoil during the winter months an advantage for people in ancient times?

2. What are the medicinal qualities that make onions good for us to eat?

3. Onions were a religious symbol for the ancient Egyptians. As well as providing food, what symbolic importance do you think the onion had for Stanley and Zero?

READING CHECK

a. Why is the lowly onion now a favorite ingredient in many recipes?

b. Why did the ancient Egyptians worship the onion?

c. How did people use the onion in the Middle Ages?

The Girl Who Loved the Sky

1. What is it that makes the girls best friends?

2. A **simile** compares two different things using the words *like, as, than,* or *resembles.* Find at least two similes in the poem.

3. A **metaphor** compares two different things by saying the one is the other. Find two metaphors in the poem.

4. What was it that the speaker in the poem didn't understand?

5. How do you think the two friends in this poem are like Stanley and Zero, and how are they different?

READING CHECK

a. The speaker in the poem is in what grade at school?

b. How does the sky taste to the blind girl?

c. The speaker in the poem states that she has no father. What do you think happened to her father?

Making Meanings

1. Why is *palindrome* a good name for this particular arrangement of words and phrases?

2. Do palindromes make use of punctuation? Explain.

3. What is a 2-D—or two-dimensional—palindrome? Try your hand at making one of these. The Greeks put a palindrome on a fountain—where will you put yours?

READING CHECK

a. Where did the word *palindrome* come from? What does it mean?

b. What is a word-unit palindrome? Make up one of your own as an example.

c. What is a mirrored palindrome? Make up your own as an example.

4. Why do you think Sachar made Stanley's name a palindrome?

Ethan Explains the B and B Inn

1. Describe the Sillington house. Do you think Mr. Singh made a good choice when he bought the house? Why or why not?

2. Why does Ethan hang back so as to be the last one off the bus?

3. How is Mrs. Olinski different from the other teachers that Ethan has had?

4. Give two examples of how the other students punish Julian for being the "strangest person to ride the bus." How does Julian respond to these examples of harassment? What do you think of his responses?

READING CHECK

a. Why does Ethan Potter feel that he has been a disappointment to every one of his teachers?

b. What is one thing about the new boy that makes him different from everyone else?

c. Why does Julian choose *Alice's Adventures in Wonderland* to issue his invitation?

d. Why has Mr. Singh brought his family to Clarion County?

5. Sillington house and Camp Green Lake are, on the surface, not at all alike. Yet for Stanley and Zero at Green Lake and Julian, Nadia, and Ethan at Sillington house, each setting helps bring about a change for the better. Explain why this is so, giving examples of events that happen in both settings to change the characters.

Making Meanings

1. How does the Gila monster use its venom?

2. Why is a low metabolic rate an advantage for the Gila monster?

3. What are the problems faced by the Gila monster?

4. Contrast and compare the Gila monster with the lizard in *Holes*.

> **READING CHECK**
>
> **a.** How has Dan Beck been able to study the Gila monster?
>
> **b.** How long has the Gila monster been around?
>
> **c.** Where does the Gila monster store energy?

The Snake King

1. Do you think you would like to work with Temba? Tell why you feel this way.

2. What clues tell you that the country Temba enters when he emerges from the passage is magical? Can you think of another story where these same clues are used?

3. Why does the Snake King agree to help Temba find his way back home?

4. Do you think Temba is right to refuse to tell the way to the snakes' kingdom? What are the results of his refusal?

5. A fable is a story that contains a lesson. What do you think is the lesson in this fable?

6. In what ways is the story of Snake King like *Holes*? In what way is it different? Give examples of at least three symbols that appear in both of the stories.

> **READING CHECK**
>
> **a.** What do Temba and the other woodcutters discover in the ground?
>
> **b.** Why do the lads leave Temba in the hole?
>
> **c.** How does Temba get out of the hole?
>
> **d.** What does Temba promise the Snake King?
>
> **e.** What is the only cure for the Chief's sickness?

Name _____ Date _____

TEST   PART I: OBJECTIVE QUESTIONS

In the space provided, mark each true statement *T* and each false statement *F.*
(10 points)

_____ **1.** Camp Green Lake is really a work camp for bad boys.

_____ **2.** Stanley and the other boys must run back and forth across the lake bed every day.

_____ **3.** Stanley blames all of his bad luck on his father, an inventor.

_____ **4.** Kissin' Kate Barlow was once Green Lake's teacher, Miss Katherine.

_____ **5.** Zero teaches Stanley to read.

**Complete each statement by writing the letter of the best answer in the
space provided. *(10 points)***

  6. Madame Zeroni tells Elya Yelnats to carry a _____ up the mountain.
    a. goat   **b.** child   **c.** pig

  7. Clyde "Sweet Feet" Livingston donated the _____ that Stanley was accused of stealing.
    a. sneakers   **b.** baseball bat   **c.** sugar

  8. Stanley tries to escape from camp in a _____.
    a. horse trailer   **b.** water truck   **c.** school bus

  9. Stanley and Zero find refuge on _____.
    a. a mountain   **b.** an island   **c.** a rooftop

 10. The Warden, Mr. Sir, and Mr. Pendanski watch as _____ crawl on Stanley and Zero.
    a. spiders   **b.** snakes   **c.** lizards

**Finish each statement by writing the letter of the best answer in the space
provided. *(10 points)***

_____ **11.** Charles "Trout" Walker's nickname refers to his —
    a. love of fishing   **b.** smelly feet   **c.** taste for seafood

_____ **12.** The Warden makes the boys dig —
    a. to find treasure   **b.** for the exercise   **c.** after sundown

_____ **13.** Stanley and Zero survive by eating —
    a. grass   **b.** cactus   **c.** onions

_____ **14.** The Warden makes her fingernails dangerous with —
    a. a file   **b.** rattlesnake venom   **c.** metal tips

_____ **15.** Zero confesses that it was he who —
    a. ate the sunflower seeds   **b.** stole the sneakers   **c.** found the lipstick container

TEST   PART II: SHORT-ANSWER QUESTIONS

Answer each question using the lines provided. *(40 points)*

16. How is Stanley treated by the teachers and students at his school?

_____

_____

_____

17. Why is Mr. Sir so sure that Stanley will not run away?

_____

_____

_____

18. When does Miss Katherine fall in love, and with whom?

_____

_____

_____

19. Why does Miss Katherine become an outlaw?

_____

_____

_____

20. What do Clyde Livingston's shoes, the Yelnatses' apartment, and Stanley's cot all have in common?

_____

_____

_____

TEST PART II: SHORT-ANSWER QUESTIONS *(cont.)*

21. What is God's thumb?

_____

_____

_____

22. Why doesn't Hector Zeroni's nickname, Zero, fit him?

_____

_____

_____

23. How do the other boys at the camp react to Zero helping Stanley dig?

_____

_____

_____

24. How does the Warden react when she discovers that Zero has run away?

_____

_____

_____

25. How do Stanley and Zero finally make it out of the hole with the suitcase?

_____

_____

_____

TEST PART III: ESSAY QUESTIONS

Choose _two_ of the following topics. Use your own paper to write two or three paragraphs about each topic you choose. _(30 points)_

1. How does Stanley change over the course of the novel? Tell what Stanley is like at the beginning of the novel, outline the changes that occur, and describe Stanley at the end of the story. Give examples of each stage of Stanley's development.

2. One theme in _Holes_ is that optimism and perseverance pay off. Discuss how this theme is reflected in Stanley's life.

3. The difference between expectation and reality creates twists in the plot of _Holes_ and provides much of the humor. Give at least three examples of irony from the book, and explain why each example is ironic.

4. Stanley discovers many connections between his ancestors' lives and his own. Discuss the similarities between Stanley's life and the life of his great-great-grandfather, Elya Yelnats. Then, explore actions taken by Elya that end up affecting Stanley many years later.

5. Discuss how one of the **Connections** from the back of the HRW LIBRARY edition of the novel is related to a theme, issue, or character in _Holes_.

Use this space to make notes.

Answer Key

Answer Key

Part One

■ Making Meanings

> **READING CHECK**
>
> **a.** Camp Green Lake, technically a juvenile correctional facility, is a work camp for bad boys located in a vast, dry lake bed in Texas.
>
> **b.** Stanley and the other boys who are inmates at Camp Green Lake are forced to dig one hole every single day of the week. Each hole must be five feet deep and five feet wide.
>
> **c.** An Egyptian woman cursed Elya Yelnats for breaking a promise to carry her up a mountain. Stanley's family doesn't really believe in the curse, but it makes them feel better to have someone to blame.
>
> **d.** Stanley writes his mother of fictitious events because he doesn't want his parents to worry about him.
>
> **e.** Zero offers to exchange his help digging Stanley's daily hole for Stanley's help teaching Zero to read.
>
> **f.** Miss Katherine had fallen in love with Sam, the onion seller. Townspeople killed him because he kissed her. She became an outlaw to avenge his death.

1. Students may mention that Stanley takes his wrongful conviction without much argument. He does not put up resistance, even when he is being picked on. He even lies about the camp to his mother to make it easier on her. Students might say they would tend to fight back more and be angrier about the situation.

2. Stanley must overcome his physical weakness to dig his holes in the baked ground under the hot sun. By digging the holes, Stanley becomes physically and mentally strong enough to face the challenges that await him.

3. Elya wanted to marry a girl named Myra, and he needed a fat pig to give her father. If Elya carried the piglet to the stream every day, as it grew big and fat, Elya would grow stronger. Madame Zeroni knew that Elya would then be strong enough to keep the promise he had made to her

in return for the piglet and the advice. He would be strong enough to carry her up the mountain to the stream, too.

4. Mostly, Sachar invokes the sense of smell for things with an unpleasant odor: Clyde Livingston's shoes, Stanley's parents' apartment, his cot at camp, his cereal (which smells like his cot), Trout Walker's feet, and onions. Only occasionally do things smell good, like Miss Katherine's peach preserves.

5. The facility is named Camp Green Lake, but it is not a camp, it isn't green, and there has not been a lake in the area for almost a hundred years. Zero isn't really a zero. Despite being uneducated, he is actually very competent with numbers, and he learns quickly. His name is not an indication of his intelligence, but it is short for Zeroni. Ironically, he is a descendant of the gypsy from Latvia, Madame Zeroni.

6. The nicknames are given in response to each boy's character, making it easier to remember each individual, and they provide a short description of each person. Students may suggest that the author does not have to spend much time describing each nicknamed character.

7. Over the course of Part One, Sachar uses flashbacks to introduce Elya Yelnats and the ancient family curse, as well as Miss Katherine Barlow and the original town of Green Lake. One example is when Miss Katherine, long a notorious outlaw, meets Trout Walker in a final, fatal encounter.

8. Responses will vary and need not be shared with the class.

9. Responses will vary, but may include people such as Randall Dale Adams, made famous by the 1988 documentary *The Thin Blue Line,* who was accused of and almost executed for a murder he did not commit.

10. Responses will vary. Some students may agree with the decisions, saying it is a fair trade because Stanley has to save his energy for teaching. Other students may disagree, arguing that it takes as much energy to learn as it does to teach, so Zero should not have to work harder physically than Stanley does.

■ Reading Strategies

Part One: Summarizing

Responses will vary. Sample responses are provided below.

Elya Yelnats's story: Elya Yelnats lived in Latvia. He wanted to marry a girl named Myra. Elya went to Madame Zeroni for advice. She told him to carry a pig up a mountain every day for two months, then present the pig to Myra's father. Elya also promised to carry Madame Zeroni up the mountain. However, when Myra still could not decide whether to marry Elya, Elya left the country without fulfilling his promise to Madame Zeroni. So she cursed him and his family for all eternity.

Kissin' Kate Barlow's story: Miss Katherine was the teacher in Green Lake. She fell in love with Sam, the onion seller. The townspeople were prejudiced. They killed Sam because he was black and he and Miss Katherine had kissed. Heartbroken, she took revenge and became the outlaw Kissin' Kate Barlow. She robbed many people, including Stanley's great-grandfather, whom she abandoned in the desert. Trout Walker and his wife tracked Kissin' Kate down and tried to get her to reveal where she had hidden the money, but she refused to tell them, saying they and their descendants would dig without finding it. Kate died from a lizard bite before they could torture the secret from her.

Stanley Yelnats's story: Stanley is convicted of a crime he did not commit and has to work off his sentence by digging holes at Camp Green Lake. In one of his holes, Stanley finds a lipstick holder with the initials KB on it. He gives it to X-Ray, who gets a day off for having "found" it. Later, Magnet steals Mr. Sir's sunflower seeds, and Stanley takes the blame. However, when Mr. Sir complains to the Warden, the Warden scratches Mr. Sir with her venom-tipped fingernails. Then, Stanley makes a deal with Zero, who helps him dig holes in exchange for help learning to read.

FOLLOW-UP: Students may predict that Stanley and Zero will become friends and that all the story lines will converge in the second half of the novel.

Parts Two and Three

■ Making Meanings

READING CHECK

  a. Zero runs away into the desert after hitting Mr. Pendanski in the face with a shovel.

  b. Warden is looking for Kissin' Kate Barlow's buried treasure.

  c. Stanley tries to steal a water truck so he can rescue Zero. When that fails, he takes off after Zero on foot.

  d. Zero survives on Sploosh, as he calls the canned peaches he finds in the half-buried boat, *Mary Lou.*

  e. Zero and Stanley find refuge on God's thumb, a mountain formation where they find water to drink and onions to eat.

  f. It was Stanley's great-grandfather's suitcase, which contained stock certificates, promissory notes, and jewels.

---

1. Responses will vary. Some students may say that Stanley's perseverance at the camp and his father's perseverance with his inventions, in conjunction with their good attitudes, caused their luck to change for the better. Other students may say that by carrying Hector Zeroni up the mountain, giving him water and food, and singing the old Latvian pig lullaby, Stanley broke the ancient curse on his family and caused their luck to change.

2. Stanley is white, educated, and not physically fit enough at first to dig a hole quickly. Zero is black, not able to read, and strong enough to dig his holes very quickly. Both are smart and rather quiet, both persevere despite disadvantages, and both eventually triumph.

3. The author uses a change in the weather to hint at a change in store for Stanley, indicating that things are about to go from bad to worse.

4. Ironically, it is the destruction of Zero's files that sets him free when Ms. Morengo and the Attorney General come to the camp.

5. Responses will vary. Students may say that Stanley finally realizes that Zero is his friend and his concern overcomes his fear.

6. Stanley and Zero drink Sploosh to stay alive, but the peaches make Zero very ill. The boys head toward God's thumb, and when Zero collapses, Stanley carries him to the top. They survive on dirty water and onions, and when they regain their strength, they return to the hole where Stanley found the lipstick tube. While Stanley digs up the suitcase full of treasure, Zero sneaks back to camp for food.

7. Ms. Morengo, Stanley's dad's patent attorney, showed up with the Texas attorney general and shut the camp down. Stanley and Zero escape being bitten by the lizards because of all the onions they have eaten.

8. Responses will vary and need not be shared.

9. Responses will vary. Some students may say that mutual helpfulness is a good basis for a friendship because each has given as well as received. Accept any reasonable example drawn from contemporary news items, from movies and TV programs, or from literature.

10. Responses will vary. Some students will say the ending is satisfying, but others may argue that it is unrealistic and say that the story should have ended differently.

■ Reading Strategies

Parts Two and Three: Drawing Conclusions

Possible responses follow.

Stay and Wait: Zero might come back; it's safer to stay at camp; Zero might already be dead; Stanley may not be able to find Zero in the desert.

Follow Zero: It is a friend's duty to help; Zero and Stanley might find refuge on God's Thumb; Zero was right to run away.

FOLLOW-UP: Students may say they would have stayed behind because the danger was too great and Zero is probably beyond help, or they may agree with Stanley's decision, saying there is a good chance of saving Zero.

Literary Elements Worksheets

■ Theme

Kissin' Kate Barlow: If she had not fallen in love with Sam, Green Lake would not have dried up and become a desert. If she had not robbed Stanley's great-grandfather, there would have been no treasure to find, and Stanley's family might have been rich all along.

Zero: If he had not stolen the shoes and put them on a parked car, Stanley would never have been arrested. If he had not run away from the camp, Stanley would never have had the opportunity to fulfill Madame Zeroni's requirements and lift the curse.

Elya Yelnats: If he had not broken his promise to Madame Zeroni, she would not have cursed him and his family.

FOLLOW-UP: If Zero's files had not been destroyed, he would not have been set free by the Attorney General at the end of the novel.

■ Irony

1. After the Attorney General shuts down the camp, the Warden is forced to sell the land it was

on. In a few years, the site will become a Girl Scout camp.

2. *Not only does Stanley end up running away, so does Zero. They both succeed in getting away.*

3. As Mr. Pendanski, Mr. Sir, and the Warden wait for the boys to be bitten by lizards, it becomes obvious that Mr. Pendanski doesn't respect Stanley at all.

4. It is Zero, a homeless child, who steals the shoes.

FOLLOW-UP: Clyde Livingston's nickname, "Sweet Feet," is ironic because his feet are actually so smelly that his wife would not even stay in the same room with his socks. X-Ray, whose nickname implies the ability to see supernaturally well, has very bad eyesight.

■ Figures of Speech: Metaphors and Similes

1. Things being compared: "He" and "mole"
Figure of speech: metaphor

2. Things being compared: "feet", "dead fish"
Figure of speech: simile

3. Things being compared: "Zero's face" and "jack-o'-lantern"
Figure of speech: simile

4. Things being compared: *"horizon" and "web"*
Figure of speech: *metaphor*

5. Things being compared: "heart" and something that can break
Figure of speech: metaphor

FOLLOW-UP: Responses will vary. Simile: "It was full of clear cool water, and it sparkled like a giant emerald in the sun." Metaphor: "It was said that Green Lake was 'heaven on earth' and that Miss Katherine's spiced peaches were 'food for the angels.'"

Vocabulary Worksheet 1

If you wish to score this worksheet, assign the point values given in parentheses.
A. *(5 points each)*

1. a. offspring   **9.** b. skillfully
2. c. hoarse   **10.** a. unwillingly
3. b. persistence   **11.** b. ridiculous
4. d. in a tired way   **12.** c. waste time
5. c. simple   **13.** c. jealously
6. a. hateful   **14.** d. conceited
7. c. faulty   **15.** b. piercing
8. d. miserable

B. *(5 points each)*
16.–20. *Responses will vary.*

Vocabulary Worksheet 2

If you wish to score this worksheet, assign the point values given in parentheses.
A. *(5 points each)*

1. b. lessen   **9.** b. cliff
2. a. challenge   **10.** d. apologetically
3. c. amazement   **11.** c. easily recognizable
4. c. distorted   **12.** a. unstable
5. d. shaking   **13.** b. stiff
6. b. raving   **14.** d. tiring
7. a. weak   **15.** c. boring
8. c. height

B. *(5 points each)*
16.–20. *Responses will vary.*

Answer Key (cont.)

Exploring the Connections

■ About the Onion

> **READING CHECK**
>
> **a.** The onion is a favorite ingredient in many recipes because it adds flavor to bland dishes and can make an ordinary meal seem extraordinary.
>
> **b.** The ancient Egyptians worshipped the onion because they believed that its spherical shape and concentric rings symbolized eternity.
>
> **c.** During the Middle Ages, physicians used the onion to relieve headaches, snakebites, and the loss of hair, as well as for food.

1. People in ancient times did not have the methods of storing foods that we have now, such as refrigeration and freezing. A vegetable that would not rot during the winter meant that they had food to eat almost all year around.

2. Onions contain antioxidants that help block cancer and seem to be able to lower cholesterol. These are two modern medical applications.

3. For Stanley and Zero, the onion became a symbol of survival.

■ The Girl Who Loved the Sky

> **READING CHECK**
>
> **a.** The speaker in the poem is in the second grade.
>
> **b.** For the blind girl, the sky tastes like cold metal when it rains.
>
> **c.** It would seem that the father abandoned the little girl because she talks about the sky backing away from her "like a departing father."[1]

1. The girls are friends because the speaker has no father and the blind girl has no eyes.

2. Similes in the poem are: "room smelled like glue," "sky tasted like cold metal when it rained," "sky falling like chalk dust."[1]

3. Metaphors in the poem are: "tree blossomed into purple lanterns," "bruised petals of her lids," "cool umbrellas of clouds," "the sky backed away," and "my fist was another lantern."[1]

4. The speaker did not understand that for the blind girl, her blindness was a natural thing and that the two had been friends not because of a deficiency, but because they shared the world together.

5. The two friends in this poem are parted at the end; Stanley and Zero can go on being friends.

■ What are Palindromes?

> **READING CHECK**
>
> **a.** The word *palindrome* comes from the Greek *palin-dromos*, which means "running back again."
>
> **b.** In a word-unit palindrome, the words form the same sentence when read in either direction. Examples should fulfill this requirement as well as make sense.
>
> **c.** A mirrored palindrome is one in which the letters are mirror images of one another. Examples should fulfill this requirement and make sense.

1. *Palindrome* is a good word for this particular arrangement of letters and words because they must run backward in exactly the same way that they run forward—in other words, they are reversible, which is "running backward."

2. Palindromes must, in order to make sense, do away with punctuation.

3. A two-dimensional palindrome reads horizontally and vertically, that is, through two dimensions. The example should do this and make sense. Accept any reasonable attempt and explanation as to where it will be applied.

4. Stanley Yelnats's name is symbolic of his story, which runs backward and forward through time and in some ways repeats itself, reflecting the mechanics of the curse.

[1]From "The Girl Who Loved the Sky" from *At the Helm of Twilight,* by **Anita Endrezze.** Copyright © 1988 by Anita Endrezze. Reprinted by permission of the author.

■ Ethan Explains the B and B Inn

READING CHECK

a. Because Ethan Potter feels that he cannot live up to the example set by his brother, Lucas, he assumes that he has been a disappointment to all his teachers.

b. The new boy wears shorts and knee socks, he has a leather book bag, he has a British accent, his skin is dark, and he holds out his hand when he introduces himself.

c. Julian is having a tea party, and a tea party is described in that book.

d. Mr. Singh, a chef on a cruise ship, decided his family needed to settle down. He wants to turn Sillington house into a bed-and-breakfast.

1. The Sillington house is very large with a number of add-ons. It has a wraparound veranda and gingerbread trim. The main feature is a big dining room on the ground floor, and there are many rooms for guests. The house will accommodate many people comfortably. Mr. Singh made a good choice.

2. Ethan hangs back so that he can walk into school alone.

3. Mrs. Olinski is different from the other teachers because she is a paraplegic and teaches from a wheelchair.

4. The students try to trip him when he walks down the aisle of the bus, but Julian is able to force them to pull their legs in. They imitate Julian's British accent, but Julian says and does nothing. One of the boys takes Julian's book bag and writes on it. Julian changes the insulting words into a positive statement.

5. For Stanley and Zero, the harsh environment at Camp Green Lake forces them to develop both a physical and mental strength and to work together to save their lives. For Julian, Nadia, and Ethan, Sillington house gives them a refuge where they are able to become more than they were before without embarrassment.

■ Modern Science Takes a Look at an Ancient Monster

READING CHECK

a. Dan Beck has been able to study the Gila monster by using a miniature, temperature-sensing radio transmitter that is inserted in the body of the monster.

b. The Gila monster is a prehistoric creature, a contemporary of the dinosaurs.

c. The Gila monster stores energy in its tail.

1. The Gila monster produces venom when it bites down and compresses poison glands in the lower jaw. The venom travels up along grooves in the teeth and acts on the nerves of the prey. It appears that Gila monsters use their venom for defense rather than for killing for food.

2. A low metabolic rate means that the Gila monster does not have to spend a lot of time hunting for food and can spend most of its time underground where it is safe.

3. The Gila monster is a target for the illegal pet trade and is in danger of losing its habitat due to the expansion of towns and cities.

4. The lizard in *Holes* is capable of killing a person, whereas there is no record of a Gila monster killing people. Both creatures live in the desert.

■ The Snake King

READING CHECK

a. Temba and the other woodcutters discover a pit filled with honey.

b. The lads remember how Temba teased them about being slow at their work and want to manage the woodcutting without him. Later, Temba decides that they were jealous of him.

c. Temba gets out of the pit by discovering the passage used by the scorpion.

d. Temba promises the Snake King that whatever happens, Temba will not harm the King.

e. The only cure for the Chief's sickness is the heart of the Snake King.

1. Responses will vary. Some students will say that because Temba tells the truth and keeps his promises, they would like to work with him. Others may feel that Temba is too good to be true. Another observation may be that Temba is not a real person but a symbolic person who represents a certain way of living.

2. Clues that tell the reader that the place where Temba emerges from the passage is magical are: There are unusual trees, flowers and shrubs; the house has a golden door with a golden latch fastened with a silver peg; the room he enters is beautifully and richly furnished; and the snakes who enter the room are dressed as people. Students may mention *Alice's Adventures in Wonderland* and the door at the bottom of the rabbit hole that opens into Wonderland. Accept any reasonable example in which one or more of the magical qualities are present.

3. The Snake King agrees to help Temba because Temba has never tried to harm the King's subjects. He is also sympathetic to Temba's situation and believes Temba's story.

4. Students should agree that Temba is right to refuse to betray the Snake King because he has made a promise and that it is important to keep promises made to friends. In the end, his refusal leads to a cure for the Chief and the rebirth of the Snake King.

5. The lesson in this story is that a person must remain true to a friend in order to have a happy life.

6. Both *Holes* and "The Snake King" are fables and contain symbolic elements that are alike: the honey pit and the treasure hole; the snakes and the scorpions; the friendship between Stanley and Zero and the bond between the Snake King and Temba. The main differences are that *Holes* is more realistic than The Snake King, and has intertwining story lines, and the story lines are set in well-defined time periods.

Test

■ Part I: Objective Questions

1. T	**9.** a. a mountain
2. F	**10.** c. lizards
3. F	**11.** b. smelly feet
4. T	**12.** a. to find treasure
5. F	**13.** c. onions
6. c. pig	**14.** b. rattlesnake venom
7. a. sneakers	**15.** b. stole the sneakers
8. b. water truck	

■ Part II: Short-Answer Questions

16. Students pick on Stanley and teachers make cruel, if unintended, remarks about his weight.

17. The camp is located a hundred miles from water in the middle of a parched lake bed. No one who runs away can survive very long.

18. Miss Katherine gradually falls in love with Sam when he repairs the schoolhouse.

19. Miss Katherine is devastated by the death of Sam, the man she loved, who was killed by residents of Green Lake.

20. They are all very smelly.

21. It is the mountain, shaped like a giant thumbs-up, where Stanley's great-grandfather found refuge after being robbed by Kissin' Kate. Later, Stanley and Zero find water and onions there, which help them to survive.

22. Even though Zero cannot read, he's not a zero. He is very bright, he catches on quickly, and he's good with numbers. He is also a good and loyal friend.

23. The boys get angry and taunt Stanley. They call Zero Stanley's slave. Eventually one of the boys, Zigzag, picks a fight.

24. The Warden does not care about Zero's safety. She orders Mr. Pendanski and Mr. Sir to destroy all of Zero's files so it will look like Zero was never even at the camp.

25. The Attorney General shows up with Stanley's father's patent attorney and gets both boys released. The lizards do not bite the boys because of all the onions they ate.

■ Part III: Essay Questions

1. Stanley begins the novel as an overweight, friendless boy from a poor family who is falsely branded a thief. Bullies like Derrick Dunne torment Stanley, and the teachers do not take the problem seriously because Stanley is bigger. He's so big, in fact, that he ends up being the butt of jokes by both students and teachers. Stanley begins to change at the camp. At first he can barely finish his hole. However, he becomes stronger physically as he digs his holes each day. The boys at camp give him a nickname, showing that they accept him, and Stanley even makes a friend. He gains new self-confidence when he takes the initiative and follows his friend into the desert to save him. In the end, Stanley triumphs. He is rich, he is fit, he has cleared his name, and he has a new best friend.

2. Even though Stanley is convicted of and punished for a crime he did not commit, he never really loses hope or even develops a bad attitude. He perseveres, putting effort into digging his daily holes, even though it seems futile. That effort eventually pays off in two ways. He finds the lipstick container, which leads him to the treasure, and he becomes much stronger and more fit because of the exercise. Stanley's perseverance pays off again in the second part of the novel. Despite the heat and lack of water, he finds his friend Zero and carries him up the mountain. The act not only saves Zero's life, but also helps fulfill the promise Elya Yelnats made Madame Zeroni long ago.

3. There are many instances of irony for students to choose from. Sachar begins ironically, setting the story at Camp Green Lake, which is neither a camp, nor green, nor even a lake. Clyde Livingston testifies that the stolen sneakers were his and says that whoever stole them from homeless children is a horrible person. Ironically, it is Zero, a homeless child, who steals the shoes. Clyde Livingston's nickname, "Sweet Feet," is ironic because his feet are actually so smelly that his wife cannot even stay in the same room with his socks. Other characters' names are ironic as well. X-Ray, for example, has very bad eyesight. And Hector Zeroni, nicknamed Zero because he supposedly has nothing in his head, is really very bright. As an inmate, Stanley finds it ironic that he once thought that he wanted to work for the FBI. The Warden has all of Zero's files destroyed so that when he dies of thirst in the desert, no one will come looking for him. Ironically, it is this act that sets him free when Ms. Morengo and the Attorney General come to the camp. And at the end of the novel, the author reveals that

Camp Green Lake will soon be a Girl Scout camp, ironic because Mr. Sir liked to taunt the boys by saying, "This isn't a Girl Scout camp."

4. Stanley has many connections with his great-great-grandfather. Like him, Stanley becomes stronger through hard work. Both persevere despite the circumstances. However, if Elya had not broken his promise to Madame Zeroni, she wouldn't have cursed him and his family, and Stanley might never have ended up at Camp Green Lake. By carrying Zero up the mountain, Stanley fulfills the promise that his great-great-grandfather did not.

5. Responses will vary according to class interaction with the **Connections** selections.